# Thoughts of an Autistic Mom

Veronica Doleman

Presentation by *BookLeaf Publishing*

Web: www.bookleafpub.com

E-mail: info@bookleafpub.com

ISBN: 978-93-95890-33-5

First edition 2022

# DEDICATION

To my younger self: The kid who didn't understand why they didn't belong anywhere: you'll find yourself eventually and you will inspire others to find themselves too. Keep wandering little one.

To my little potato: You completed changed my life from the moment those two little lines appeared. Looking forward to seeing where we wander together!

# ACKNOWLEDGEMENT

Husband: I have evolved and changed so much in the last 18 years we have been together. I appreciate that you are a little more steady and the true foundation of our relationship. Thank you for accepting me for who I am, even when who that is seems to change pretty regularly. I am so happy we are now embarking on the journey of parenthood together; I wouldn't want to do it with anyone else.

I would like to thank the numerous autistic creators who share their traits and interests. I wouldn't have figured out I was autistic without your vulnerability and I am so grateful. To the folks in the weekly autism support group; thank you so much. I can't make it to many meetings anymore with the baby but you made my diagnosis journey so much better and I truly value our conversations.

# PREFACE

I found myself lost after having my baby. Between breastfeeding, bedsharing, and my husband going back to shift work, I wasn't sure who I was anymore. My spare moments were taken up by tiktoks and reels; anything that I could watch muted with one free hand as my baby slept on me. By the end of the day, my eyes would hurt from staring at the screen. Six months before I had the baby, I received my autism diagnosis after self-diagnosing a year prior. This information changed how I viewed myself and would impact me so much as a mother.

I decided I would complete this 21 day writing challenge as a way to go back to something I loved when I was younger. Teenage Veronica had books upon books of poetry and songs. Writing made me so happy. I had many different journals where I would document my life. When I went to University I quickly found out I was not up to par and it took the joy of writing from me. This is a way for me to put some of my thoughts out there without worrying if it is good enough. For the first time in years, I look forward to the quiet time alone in the evening when I can write. I am putting down the screen and putting pen to paper. It feels amazing. I hope you enjoy this little glimpse into my world.

# Mommy

I did not think since giving birth
That I would have to pack weeks' worth
Of stuff to simply leave my hearth
But I'm a mommy.

I never thought I'd sit with poop
On me while singing on a loop
Not worried how my tum does droop
Guess I'm a mommy.

I never thought that I would share
My breasts in public without care
And wear such frumpy underwear
But I'm a mommy

I always thought that I would show
My baby as they change and grow
Instead I share a potato
Protective mommy.

I never thought I'd pick a nose
Or clean out jam from little toes
Let someone spit up on my clothes
But I'm a mommy.

Pooping has become a chore
Pee drips when at the bathroom door
I'm working on my pelvic floor
Perks of a mommy.

I never thought that I'd tiptoe
Around the house and only go
To sleep with an infant's say so
But I'm a mommy.

Those hugs that fit me like a glove
The giggles when held up above
I never knew this kind of love
Grateful I'm Mommy.

# Labels

drAmatic
manipUlative
inTimidating
prIncess
pSycho
disrespecTful
connIving
piCky

# Who Am I?

I spent my whole life absorbing traits from others.

I wonder if that's why I always chose Kirby in Smash Bros.

I remember people thinking I was mocking their accents when I didn't even notice the change myself.

I find myself at 34, not entirely sure of who I am.

What are parts of me and what parts were borrowed from others?

What do I actually like to do?

When I'm asked what makes my heart sing, I usually just cry.

Where do I start to get to know the real me?

I think the answer lies in little me; Little Veronica. Connecting with my inner child.

Allowing those things that others scorned and criticized to bring me joy once again.

Before it is too late. Before that kid disappears forever.

# Yours

On the day you were born, I became something new.

A transformation which in certain moments I didn't think I could survive.

Starting with small, building waves.

It came over and over until I felt I was breaking open.

In a way I was.

I think back and see myself as if in a movie.

My body taking over. My mind not getting a chance to doubt that this is happening.

I breathed you out of me. In the presence of only your Daddy. What a joy. What a moment.

I held you first. Lifted you from the water and I was yours.

We rejoiced, speaking the name we kept close to our hearts for so long. Yours.

The fear. The unknown. The pain. It ended so abruptly.

You are here.

I am forever changed.

# Tarot Poem

My three cards: Ace of Swords, Page of Wands Reversed, Two of Wands

The fog wraps tightly around your feet.
The dance between alert and anxious.
Eager to start the journey, but weary of the road ahead.

The path is one to start alone. Tell no one of your departure.
Your past can pull at you like a ball and chain.
Or it can be the flames licking at your heels that get you to start.

That gnawing in your gut? A warning.
Do not heed the doubt.

One step at a time.

Make your choice.

Try it!
You can try writing your own tarot poem. Sit with your deck, set the intention, pull three cards. As you look at the cards, write and see

what is born. Feel free to use the imagery, look up meanings, or follow your intuition. There is no right or wrong way.

Feel free to share your poem with me! (tag @yourwanderingguide on Instagram)

# Hyperlexic

These are words I mispronounced the first time I said them outloud.

Tuscon
agate
bedraggled
Penelope
duodenum
awry

Some uttered in a safe space where I was quietly corrected.

Some said where I was shamed and ridiculed.

I remember the feeling of my face growing hot.
And urge myself to be the safe space for others.

# Choke

In ancient times, my body would be worshipped.

There are statues and idols where I see my shape
and curves.

A celebration of what it can do.

Now I am expected to do it all
While shrinking
While taking less space
While fading

Fighting those expectations
Rebellion through simple existence

Forcing them to see me. All of me.

If they don't like it, they can choke on it.

# Meltdowns

I remember learning a meltdown can be
emotional.

A lightbulb went off in my head.

Times where I couldn't control my laughter.
Outside a playful grin. Inside I was the joker, the
smile stretched over a pained grimace.

Times when my embarrassment would result in
blows and shrieks.

Times when the sobbing would render me
speechless.

The hot tears of anger in a work meeting

All interpreted as a childish outburst.
Met with discipline, shock, or jeers.

Spoiled.
Unprofessional.
Crazy.
Inappropriate.

In reality...

Overwhelmed.
Misunderstood.
At her limit.
A cry for help.

# Missing

I would swear to myself that today will be the
day I would go outside.

That I would put down the phone and sit in
nature.

That I would slow down and appreciate where I
was in the moment.

Every day the same disappointment. The sun set
and my face was lit up by a blue light.

I think it began to suck my soul from my eyes.

The world seemed dim compared to the colorful,
curated squares.

I was fading away.

Then you came.

Now each day we sit outside together.
Hearing the breeze ripple through the trees.

Feeling the warmth of the sun on our cheeks.
Finding beauty in the simple day to day.

I marvel, because all I was missing was you.

# 18 Years: A Haiku

I know you hate it

When I share things about you

So I'll stop right here

# Anger

Shove it down.
Shout it out.
Take it out on someone smaller.

Seethe and stew.
Pen rips paper.
Just wait til I am taller.

Didn't know.
Could be clues.
To show me what I needed.

Stand up now.
Sit this one out.
How I should be treated.

Grown up now.
Unlearn I must.
The pause has got me thinking.

Family curse.
So much hurt.
The chains we are unlinking.

# Join Us!

Pssst. Hey you.

Did you feel like an alien growing up? Like you never really belonged anywhere?

Were you a whiny kid who had a lot of temper tantrums (according to the adults)?

Did you grow up to have anxiety?

Do social situations make you feel sick or exhausted?

Did you ever sit in a psychiatrist's office with tears in your eyes after pouring your heart and soul out only to be met with "Well, you have aspects of ADHD, OCD, and anxiety. But I would only diagnose you with low self-esteem"(maybe this one is too specific)?

Do you have sensitivities to fabrics, sounds, temperature, textures, or tastes?

Do you have special rituals or routines you like to follow regularly?

If a number of these resonated with you and you are curious, consider doing some autism screening tests (I like embrace-autism.com).

You might be neurodivergent.

# Motherhood

I've never really been good at slowing down.

Always busy. Job. Side hustles. Volunteering.

Even in motherhood I'm struggling to pause.

Thinking I need to view this new role as a job.

Asking for burn out.

Rethinking the need.
Productivity.
Monetizing.
Comparison.

Enjoy having nothing to do but be with my baby.

Just try being mom.

# Liked

It is hitting now.
Uncertainty.
Pit in my stomach.

What were you thinking?
You can't write.
Who will read this?
These aren't poems, just word vomit.

The only way to silence this monster inside.
Keep putting pen to paper.
If no one reads it.
I'll survive.

# Helicopter

A seed floats down by my baby's head, twirling like a helicopter blade.

I'm reminded of how I used to love them as a child.

Throwing them up as high as I could and watching them spin to the ground.

Trying to recreate them with paper but never getting the design quite right.

Sometimes you just can't compete with nature.

I wonder if later on, they'll love them too.

# Friends

Adulting is hard, we'll say with a grin.
Though tears seem to always be close from within.
Schedules clash, busy lives, try to stay connected.
But sometimes the simple group chat gets neglected.
Each of us worried to share our struggles.
Thinking the others have much bigger troubles.
But maybe what we need is our community.
And realize we won't put each other under scrutiny.
Speaking our worries and problems outloud.
Not thinking about being weak or too proud.
Our time to decide: break these curses or keep.
Share the good and the bad, when we're losing sleep.
Taking the leap and reaching out to our group.
Connecting so we all can be kept in the loop.
Therapy, big changes, mental illness, meds.
Faced alone these challenges can be things one dreads.
With connection, caring, understanding, and love.
We can help one another to keep rising above.

Now don't be mistaken, let's still share our
dreams.
And an overabundance of tiktoks and cat
memes.

# Filter

Sometimes I keep the lamp on a little longer to watch you sleep.

I am tempted to take a picture, but I know the camera will never capture what I see.

Love is a wild filter.

# Love

I used to think I wanted loud love.
The chocolates and roses love.
On special days love.
The social media posts like novellas love.
The in-your-face love.
The fiery, burning bright love.
The big fights love.
The bigger makeups love.
The as seen on TV love.

And maybe for a time I did.

Now I find myself in quiet love.
The cotton candy and carnations love.
On any day love.
Keep it to ourselves love.
The by-your-side love.
The smoldering, cooking coals love.
The little disagreements love.
The melt when I watch you with our baby love.
The only we could write this love.

And it is all I'll ever want again.

# Village

There are times when my brain tries to trick me.

It tells me I am alone in this and that I don't have
a village.

It gets me wondering if a village even exists
anymore.

The loneliness gets overwhelming.

I get jealous of others' villages.

I build walls.

Then someone checks in.
Someone reaches out.
Someone thinks of me.

Suddenly I am not so lonely.

Maybe my definition of a village needs a tweak.

# Tarot Poem #2

My cards: Seven of Cups Reversed, Six of
Pentacles, The Tower

So many options.
Fear of making the wrong choice.
Breathe, assess, and choose.

Be creative in how you bestow gifts.
Don't give more than you think you'll receive or
you will go without.

This will be a painful experience.
The transformation will be great.
Focus on getting through to the other side.

# Finished

I can't believe I had this much fun.
Writing poems, much less twenty-one.

Younger me would be so proud of us.
Sharing thoughts and moments that are precious.

She didn't know she was autistic.
Just told she was weird, intimidating, and
pessimistic.

Now I know my brain is unique.
That my way of seeing the world needs no
tweak.

Motherhood has been the most exciting
adventure.
I never knew I could be so tender.

Taking time each night to reflect and write.
Showed me I can take time to feel light.

Doing things that fill me with joy and laughter.
Outside of being a mother and wife here after.

Lots of this came from my heart.
I am grateful to practice this art.

You've made it this far, thanks for the read.
Twenty-one poems, and a mom's mind freed.